THE PORCUPINE OF MIND

To Alyssa & Jeff
with joy & best
wishes!

love
Katerina
5/10/2012

BOOKS BY KATERINA STOYKOVA-KLEMER

The Air around the Butterfly (Bilingual)
The Most (English, chapbook)
Indivisible Number (Bulgarian)
The Porcupine of Mind (English)

EDITED BY KATERINA STOYKOVA-KLEMER

Bigger Than They Appear:
Anthology of Very Short Poems

THE PORCUPINE OF MIND

Poems by

Katerina Stoykova-Klemer

BROADSTONE BOOKS

Cover art: 'Cactus Man'
by Odilon Redon

Design and typesetting by Jonathan Greene

Library of Congress Control Number: 2012934598

ISBN 978-1-937968-00-7

Broadstone Books
An Imprint of
Broadstone Media LLC
418 Ann Street
Frankfort, KY
40601-1929
BroadstoneBooks.com

CONTENTS

O & I

O & I   3

I enjoy your company   5

ONE SHOULD EXERCISE CAUTION   6

KISSING THE SHELL OF AN EGG   7

TO THE ROCK   8

WHEN YOU KISS A GRAPE   9

How long have you been like this?   11

THE NEIGHBOR   12

KISSING THE TIDE, AS IT PULLS BACK   13

A butterfly and I   14

MOUSE MONOLOGUE   15

Wear me, said the word lifesaver   16

THE KISS OF THE STONE   17

AN HOUR AFTER   18

THE SUPERHERO IS MOVING OUT   19

THE SUITCASE   21

LULLABY   22

Don't you ever get tired of being   23

THE FLY IN MY ROOM   24

TO THE ROW OF TALL CANDLES IN THE STORE   26

How did you get to be so beautiful   27

CUMULATIVE   28

LOVE HAS EVERYTHING   29

KISSING A SNOWMAN   30

THE VISITOR   31

KISSING THE LIPS OF REALLY BAD NEWS   33

THE MOST   34

So, what did you learn?   35

TWO   36

IN THE WATER, UNDER THE BRIDGE   37

YOUR FATE WHISPERED IN YOUR EAR   38

Dear   39

THE HUG   40

OPTIMISTIC   41

PESSIMISTIC   42

TO MY HULA HOOP   43

THE ENDING OF SLAVIC NAMES

YOU'LL NEVER PRONOUNCE THE WORD   47

My name is OV,   48

BETTER   49

DREAMS,   51

CREATIVE SPURT   52

MY TONGUE, MY ENEMY   53

MOTHER AND SON IMMIGRANTS   54

Do you mean   55

CYRILLIC LETTERS   56

THE PULL OF ONE'S ORIGIN   57

SHE-WOLF IN A BUFFALO HIDE   58

MERMAID IN THE CORNFIELD   59

WHAT HAPPENS TO THE PROPHET   61

VISIT   62

THE DOWNSIDE OF LUCIDITY

I respond to kindness   65

SKIN,   66

GUILT,   67

UNFORGIVENESS,   68

HATE   69

THE STONE   70

THE CLAM   71

I pictured you younger,   72

SURPRISE   73

EXTRAVAGANCE   74

RETIREES IN THE GYM   75

THE ARTIST   77

HOPE   78

MOTH WOMAN,   79

THE WAY I USED TO PRAY TO ST. CATHERINE   80

I am dark and damp and scared   81

NOTICE   82

CLARIFICATION   83

DRIVE-BY COMMODES   84

I ate seventeen apples today,   85

THE FISH, THE NET, AND THE FISHERMAN   86

THE CONVERSATION   86

Why do you breathe   89

SU   90

Beneath the skull—locked door   91

TO THE BUGS STILL DROWNING IN THE POOL   92

Thinking of the water   93

SOBRIETY,   94

WORRY DOLLS   95

Have you ever seen   97

YOU AND KARMA   98

FOOD   99

NOTES   101

ACKNOWLEDGMENTS   102

O & I

O & I

His name is O.

He is a single cell
organism and my closest friend.

We met last winter.
I was about to step

on him when I noticed
his milky body

and picked it up
from the concrete.

Ha! I said, while I observed
him on my palm.

Whew! he said when he figured
that I meant no harm.

Well? I said, when gently
I dropped him in my wallet.

OK! He snuggled
between a photo and a dollar.

3

That evening, I placed him
in a glass of water by my bed.

He pressed his tummy flat
against the glass and didn't take

his eye off me until next morning
when I opened mine and saw him

smiling. He stared down at his mitochondria,
but his ribosomes blushed pink.

You mean the world to me, I told him.

I enjoy your company,
smiled *Host.*
I can't imagine life
without you, admitted *Parasite.*

ONE SHOULD EXERCISE CAUTION

when kissing a daffodil.
Somebody could get hurt.
It helps to have dabbled in botany.
To reach the Sweet of Hearts
without splitting apart her innermost
petals is a high art. While the kiss lasts,
you'll share her crown.
You'll shimmer in the sun for days
after you drift apart.

KISSING THE SHELL OF AN EGG

Rock with a secret, I like your cool
firmament, the predictable
closure of nutrients, the smooth
packaging. You taste of surface,
feel like a moon, hiding
the inner sky's weather,
wings or scales.

TO THE ROCK

Eventually
there will be a plant
whose root you won't
be able to resist, and
you'll let it in,
first soft and white,
tender as an earthworm.
You will open your
self to its quiet knocks
as it starts traveling through you
on its way to the earth,
on its way to the juice
it really craves.
As it plummets
through your lungs,
you will hang
on it like an old ring,
a shriveled pearl
at the tip of a tongue,
a raisin, on its way to dust.

WHEN YOU KISS A GRAPE

you are his
whole world. Your tongue
surrounds him
as if he were hard
candy. The two of you work
as partners. You are the one
supplying the wet,
he brings in you the sweet.
You roll him
from tooth to tooth,
he bounces off—
a football with taut skin.
The tiny opening where
the stem used to cord him
to the mothership
leaks sticky juice.
You close your eyes
and your teeth;
his body cleaves.
Then you understand
he's always been the one
more vulnerable.
You wish him
whole again, but

it's too late now. Too
impossible. Still,
he is yours to keep, yours
to swallow.

How long have you been like this?
I asked the word *raisin* when I opened the box.
Hlp m! Hlp m! he yelped, and tried to cry.

THE NEIGHBOR

is picketing
a fence. So what?

He's got the right
to his own space.

So do you
in me.

So do I
in him.

We cell
ourselves.

We graze
our own

fields.

KISSING THE TIDE, AS IT PULLS BACK

Then the wind is done
being a breeze and insists
you leave the shore at once,
alone,

and for your own
good.

Then the sand
is at its heaviest.

The ocean mists
its eye and then

a wave becomes
an afterthought
of an embrace
with outstretched arms.

You stare
at your feet—one wet,
one mystified.

A butterfly and I
met on the sidewalk.

She blocked my way
with her big wings.

I stood and waited
for her to let me through.

She flew away, but I
still don't know

what to do.

MOUSE MONOLOGUE

After the science
experiment, after
the last sunflower
seed at the end
of the labyrinth,
I'm going back
home, back

to my boa.

We will snuggle
in concentric circles,
catnap for days, buried
in bedding.

Then she will sway
at me, and I will wave
my tail

with my heart
in my throat,
darting
from corner to corner.

Wear me, said the word *lifesaver*
when it floated up to me.
Think of me
as another ring.

THE KISS OF THE STONE

is slow
and significant.

Set in his ways, he knows
how he wants you
to turn your face, how much
breath to apply on his
deliberate tongue.

While your lips are locked,
you meet his gaze and see that he
already waits for you at this same spot
in at least three centuries.

That's when your next kiss
will be. That's when he'll admit
he's never stopped loving you.

He will ask your dust to marry him
back then.

AN HOUR AFTER

that repulsive growth, burnt by scarlet
medicines, finally fell off my face,
I met my future
ex-husband, and he decided

I was marvelous.

He said *I do,*
I said *I do,*
and so we did,

until a wart sprang
from his nose and grew as big
as an extra face,
grew as big
as an extra lung,
grew as big
as a Cadillac and grew much
bigger than us,
until the wart was all
I could see.

And he couldn't
see at all.

THE SUPERHERO IS MOVING OUT

In his wife's smallest suitcase
he packs:
> a toothbrush
> a change of tights.

In a long row
with boogers and tears smeared
across their cheeks,
his children stare at him.

As he approaches the door,
the stove timer goes off.

Would you like to have dinner
with us? His aproned wife
emerges from the kitchen.

For one last time, he sits
at the head of the table, his back
to the large windows with
sinister city lights.

She serves potatoes
and lamb. His favorite.

They eat in silence, while
the dishwasher hurls
water from side to side.

Do you want me to drive you
to the airport? she asks.
No, thank you, he answers. I'll fly.

THE SUITCASE

At least fifteen times a day
I think about your suitcase.
And how it takes space
lying right here, taking over
the floor of my bedroom,
gasping with outrage, gaping,
staring with its door unzipped—
a checkered, all-seeing eye.

At least fifteen times a day
I walk around your suitcase.
I step on its left
I step on what's left
of my surroundings.

At least fifteen times a day
I hate your fucking suitcase
on my floor by my door
like a hole in my room.
Lying there like a bomb
ticking

one, two, three...

All the way to fifteen.

LULLABY

Unwrinkle
your forehead,

unclench
your throat.

There'll still be misery
tomorrow,

morning-fresh,

going off with your alarm,
snaking through your toothpaste.

If you wake up,
it will move with you

like a shoe,
like a tattoo.

Don't you ever get tired of being
here? I asked the word *ghost.*
Don't you ever get tired of not being
yourself? he answered.

THE FLY IN MY ROOM

I lived with hands pressed
to my ears. I wore her
as an emerald in my hair.

At night I stayed up
and waited for her

to fall asleep,
to die,

or for me to die first.

We shared a pillow. She laid
eggs in my dreams.

I've never conceded, but
we both know that tomorrow

I'll pack my things up
and leave.

But tonight she looks at me
with honeycomb eyes,

and I track
the veins of her wings
with my ring finger

as her body
shudders and stills,
shudders and stills.

TO THE ROW OF TALL CANDLES IN THE STORE

Which one of you
skinny ladies
wants to burn
in the name of love?

How did you get to be so beautiful?
I asked the word *cynical*.
How did you get to be so stupid?
she answered.

CUMULATIVE

Gather your disappointments.
One by one, carry them in your beak,
bond them together with dirt and spit,
with contorted twigs, which twist
to make a perfect circle.
Now, lay an egg.
Now, sit there.
Sit.

LOVE HAS EVERYTHING

Sun, time, sea,
aura like a strawberry.

No, it's not silver.

Have you ever seen silver
that wasn't melted in fire
and pulled by pliers?

No, it's not crystal.

Have you ever seen crystal
that wasn't rationed into cells?

I know. I also want out.

KISSING A SNOWMAN

He loves you not.
Today—not.
Yesterday—maybe.
Tomorrow—want.
Your blood—a former drop
clings—pathetic mole
on the cheek   that used
to tender yours.
His waning face
drops   in your lap
one final   lump of coal.
He loves you   not
but loves your eye
impaled   on his carrot-sword.
You better
love him hard
and kiss him strong,
hug tight
the bulky digits
of his back,
his round base,
squeeze   the barky fingers
of his hand.
He loves you not.

A tiny drop
of melted him
seeps in between
your purple lips—
you are delivered
back to life.
He loves you not.
Under his tin-pot hat
lives only ice.

THE VISITOR

Every day, he visits her.
Every time, he brings his own cup
of ice, for she has none
in her house. She pours, he sips.
The ice cubes turn to chips,
mist, then he gets up.
Tomorrow he will bring more.

KISSING THE LIPS OF REALLY BAD NEWS

They are moist,
prepared, flat—
two volumes of the same
sad book. Hard to read,
hard to breathe, but all is clear.
Read her lips.

THE MOST

Welcome
Last Resort

We meet at last
Plan Z

I've heard a lot about you
Worst Case Scenario

I look forward to
Working with you
When-all-else-fails

It's going to be you and I now
Do you feel lucky to end up with me?

Hey, it's okay

After the initial shock
Wears off

You too
Will try to make
The most of me

So, what did you learn?
Curiosity asked the *Cat,* then
poked her carcass with a stick.

TWO

Based on Bulgarian and American adages

Two sharp stones can't
mill flour.

Two sharp bones can't
make a joint.

Two stones can break
most bones.

You can kill two birds
with one stone

or the same bird twice
with words.

IN THE WATER, UNDER THE BRIDGE

1.

I, drowning

2.

You, counting

YOUR FATE WHISPERED IN YOUR EAR

while you were playing dead
on your yoga mat.

While you were grasping the foot
of your unbending leg,
your fate came
and went
with the water under the bridge.

Don't get up.

Dear
on-again, off-again
friend,
you are welcome
to your life.
Count me in,
count me out.

THE HUG

Unsure it would be
welcomed, I pushed
the air toward him.
Our fields repelled
like two magnets—
smiling, positive.

OPTIMISTIC

Plenty of tissue left
to cry over the spilt milk.

PESSIMISTIC

The loss
of us
is a cup
too full.

I can
live like this.

TO MY HULA HOOP

Goodwill
Will be good
To you,
My sun,
My moon,
My undivided cell,
My oval pool.

O, you said,
When I stepped in-
To your ring.

O, I was so adamant
You were the final
Loop for me.

O, tidy O,
I swam
Inside your yolk,
Floated like fruit,
Flew snug
Along your rim.

O, memento mobile,
Roll towards another girl,

Dance on top of someone
Else's hips.

O, Wiedersehen

O, life
I could have been.

THE ENDING OF SLAVIC NAMES

YOU'LL NEVER PRONOUNCE THE WORD

love the same
after you've kissed
a foreigner. A few
papillae will always remain
living in her
country, whose language you've heard
a total of three times.
For years, you will pull
your L's and push your R's
to remember life
in her mouth. At times, your grammar
will skid after her footprints.
But you could never leave
that quick nor go
that far.

My name is *Ov*,
like the ending
of Slavic names.
I used to be called *Love,*
but as it turned out,
L was silent.

BETTER

for Toni

The time I left
my best friend behind

was a time of hope
for something better

than a best friend,

was a time of hope
for true love,

was a time of hope
for a better life, better

than a best friend,
better than her

true love, better

than a life
with my best friend, better

than holding hands
on busted streets, better

than sharing
the cheapest ice cream, better

than her lithe body spooning mine
in the hotel room by the U.S. consulate, better

than our unconditional love
unless I find

something better.

The time I left
my best friend behind,

there were parts of me
I left her. I left her.

DREAMS,

film strips
from the '80s,
'90s and beyond.
My time
to be a hero
didn't come
and went on.
Still,
I buy a ticket.
In the darkness
of the theater,
I feel as if
I'm staring
from every seat.

CREATIVE SPURT

By now the moon has shrunk back
to a dark comma in the sky,
and I have stopped writing.

Two weeks of rubbing pen and paper
like a cicada its front legs, and erupting
in some language I no longer use

for thinking. They say the tongue
you become a poet in is the one
which can never tell a lie.

If it leaves me now, who will miss it?
How could I live with it, without it?

MY TONGUE, MY ENEMY

Without you—blood in the mouth.
I swallow, the Latin
serifs scratch.
My tongue, my brother.
Decorated, perforated—
metal ball rolls
along the teeth like a
perverse arrowhead.
Tongue or Death.
My tongue, my own carcass.
My tongue, another friend
whom I've betrayed.
Shouldering guilt,
the innocent start running.
My tongue, my scream—
scream of shame.
My tongue, my bow—
I release you with no aim.
My tongue, my home.
Forgive me. I am gone.

MOTHER AND SON IMMIGRANTS

He cries, Mom, I have a boo boo.
She asks, What's a boo boo?

Do you mean
      corners in Bulgarian,
or
    the opposite of beautiful?
I asked the word *ugly.*
You must be blind…И глупав, she answered.

CYRILLIC LETTERS

Stacked in a row a little longer than
that of your Latin uncles and aunts,
you huddle up to keep warm.
Your parallel lines abound—
arms stretched toward the common sun.

АБВГДЕЖЗИЙКЛМНОПРСТУФХЦЧШЩЪЬЮЯ

THE PULL OF ONE'S ORIGIN

The hanged man climbs back
along his own rope.

SHE-WOLF IN A BUFFALO HIDE

roams through the prairie. Gets used to
eating grass. Becomes a leader
of a herd. It suits her to be in charge.
She likes to stop, sniff the air
and point—*walk that way.*
Or—*spend the night here and build fires*
to keep the wolves away. They are coming,
coming, so close,
I am shivering.

MERMAID IN THE CORNFIELD

We found
a mermaid in the cornfield.
Covered in mud.
Tired from dragging around her tail.
She was eating corn,
holding an ear with one hand.
With the other, she was wiping off her tears.
That's how we found her.
We followed the whimpering sounds;
we thought it was a baby animal.

Instead,
it was a mermaid in the cornfield.
Her hair, blue as the ocean,
was tangled with weeds,
dusty and dirty,
with a fish skeleton-comb to hold it in place
above her seaweed eyes.

She had bite marks of animals,
fat lip and scabs.
That's how we found her.
From far away,
she looked like a dolphin
caught in a blue net.

Instead,
it was a mermaid in the cornfield.
Ants were crowding her tail,
trying to pull a few scales
to take home for winter.
And mice were snarling,
and daring birds of prey were landing.

A few times
we asked her:
How can we help?
But she just waved her tail at us
to go away.

We did. But
it didn't feel right
to leave her there like that,
so we returned
and carried her off
in the back of the truck
to our bathtub,
where we mixed sea salt
with cold water
and dropped in it a yellow rubber duck.

WHAT HAPPENS TO THE PROPHET

who returns
to the town of his birth?

What happens to the wolf
who returns
to his own blood?

What happens to the wave
who returns
to her own sea?

What happens to the wave
who stays away?

VISIT

I visit my homeland the way a snail tries
to fit back into his old shell.
Day after day I writhe inside,
counterclockwise.

The shell is rough and narrow, opens sores
on coddled parts.

But I persist, eat tarator, cry over graves,
until I conform to my old contours. Finally,
I am here.

Snail is the most beautiful Bulgarian word,
says my son, who is studying the language.
I thought it meant *love.*

THE DOWNSIDE OF LUCIDITY

I respond to kindness
with love and joy,
confessed the word *dog*.
Please, I waved my tail,
teach me how to bark.

SKIN,

cape over my shoulders,
you are welcome to stay
with me, burn
in the sun, flap in the wind, stick
around my sorry gristle.
Do you still love me?
Would you hold my hand
as if?

GUILT,

wide-eyed beauty,
I like holding your hand.

This cigarette sends
mixed signals from the ashtray.

Next to it:
your drink, over;
your food, untouched.

Your nails are painted scarlet,
your mouth—painted shut.

UNFORGIVENESS,

splinter in your breastbone, lives
there lodged like a small tree.
Withers in winter, looms
in spring. Its fruit is sweet
on first bite, then turns
into the taste of your own flesh.

HATE

is the victim's
hunchback. It sways
like a water-
filled balloon with every step
she takes along the high bridge.
From the side, the hump
looks like an angel's wing.

THE STONE

You don't need to throw it at your enemy
for it to be a weapon.

Just warm it in your palm
while whispering his name. Imagine it a hate-

seeking missile. Picture the brisk arc,
its finding and hitting, finding and hitting;

looping for centuries. Long after
your hand is unwarm, and the fingers

loose change in your pocket,
the stone will keep on

whizzing through the air,
breaking his skull.

THE CLAM

Livid,
the clam rolled back
to the shore,
spat her pearl
on the sand,
then stormed back
to the bottom.

Let the thankless asshole
see he's nothing
without me.

She settled on her rock
and tried to yawn.

The current swayed
her jagged lips,
the boiling core,
the used-up gills.

He is nothing,
nothing, she yelled,
and choked on water.

I pictured you younger,
I told the word *naïve.*
I pictured you happier,
she answered.

SURPRISE

Under the motorcycle helmet—
a very old man.

EXTRAVAGANCE

The old man sinks
back into the hammock
of his body. *Do I
really need all this?*

RETIREES IN THE GYM

Every morning
after the first round of medication,
they arrive
with eyes full of purpose
and socks pulled high
to the knee braces.

They totter from the low back machine
to the chest press
to the leg press
to the spine twist.
Then silently abduct the hips.

Lifting the vinyl-coated dumbbells
with eyes closed,
they want to feel the muscles contract
like slugs
inside gray arms
among veins and bumps.

They want to picture the tendons
still attached to the hollowing bones.

Out of consideration for the rest of us,
they conscientiously wipe the equipment

from any old people sweat
that might have collapsed
from bald heads
or hunched backs,
while they hobbled on the treadmill,
squeezing the rail
with both hands.

THE ARTIST

for Simeon Kondev

Here are your eyes,
here are your glasses.

I put the lips
in the wrong place

and had to move them.
That's why

you have a shadow
under the left cheekbone.

Tomorrow I'll draw you again.
We won't be adding a body.

HOPE

doubles the size
of a soul.
Triples the length
of the rosary.

MOTH WOMAN,

turn off the light
and pray. In the dark

you can ask for
just about anything.

Wet, unlaid,
your eggs are listening.

Your night has come.

THE WAY I USED TO PRAY TO ST. CATHERINE

In the church,
I'd light a candle.

I'd walk up to the icon,
squat an inch

so that my eyes
aligned with hers.

I'd look at her,
she'd look at me,

and we would stay this way
until she knew everything.

I am dark and damp and scared
of myself, admitted the word *corner.*
Please, bowed the word *room,*
let me hide inside you.

NOTICE

The broken-off handle of the drawer
is in the drawer.

CLARIFICATION

The beetle

lying on his back
is not kicking in the air.

He is praying
for wind.

DRIVE-BY COMMODES

Three commodes on the curb
awaiting their rides in the garbage truck.

Two domesticated—with their lids down—
and a rebel sticking a lid up like a tongue.

Three commodes facing the street
like a suburban family
waiting for the bus downtown.

Three commodes in pretty good shape—
round where it counts,
bulging in all the right places.

Facing the street in full frontal
by a curbside and a mailbox.
Equidistant from each other.

One, waving its round arm, ready for a hug.
Two, already sleeping
with their eye lids closed.

I ate seventeen apples today, bragged *Primate*.
That's wonderful, beamed *Prime Number*
and clapped his two hands three times.

THE FISH, THE NET, AND THE FISHERMAN

Wishes s/he were an accountant

Wishes s/he were a stocking

Wishes s/he were 1/16th of the moon

Wishes s/he went to school

Wishes s/hewouldn't constantly smell like fish

Wishes s/he weren't roped into this

Wishes s/he were a dreamcatcher

Wishes this were a dream

	THE FISH	THE NET	THE FISHERMAN
			✓
		✓	
	✓		
	✓		✓
		✓	✓
	✓	✓	✓
		✓	
	✓		

THE CONVERSATION

Reluctant to talk about anything
but himself, the poet shrunk
into his cigarette.
The offensive lack of topics discussing
his plight[1] prompted
another beer.[2]

[1] latest book, influence, metamorphosis

[2] storm out, insult, demonstration

Why do you breathe
so hard? I asked.
Greatness needs more air,
answered *Pride*,
bulging like an extra chest.

su

NAME su - run a shell with substitute user and group IDs
SYNOPSIS su [OPTION]... [-] [USER [ARG]...]
DESCRIPTION Change the effective user id and group id to
that of USER.—*Linux Man Pages*

su, also known as "switch user," is a UNIX shell command
which allows the current user to assume the identity of someone else, to inhabit the system as another, with his/her asso-
ciated permissions, degrees of authority, space allotted, etc.
Typically used in debugging hard-to-describe system issues.
The administrator must become the user in order to experi-
ence the problem first hand, so that he or she can then solve
it.

> also known as
> [shapeshifting]

> also known as
> [empathy]

> also known as
> [compassion]

after Laurie Clewett

Beneath the skull—locked door.
Beneath the gullet—well.
Somebody's hiding.
Somebody's drowning.

TO THE BUGS STILL DROWNING IN THE POOL

Unsaved by me
you kick
kick
kick
with all your fuzzy feet
sticky with surface tension.

The tension between
you and me
grows with every gulp of water
you inhale
under the drooping tent
of your chlorinated wings.

Stop staring at me
with these disco-ball eyes.
Stop waving at me
with these antennae to the sky.

I only came here to swim.

Thinking of the water
Rusting in the tap
Thirst

SOBRIETY,

downside of lucidity, your sharp
estate of brainfolds hasn't lost
an hour, emotion, each regret
fresh as the farmers market's
first cucumber and with as
much juice.

The porcupine of mind
sinks to the bottom
of the labyrinth.

Here is the argument
for a drink, a joint, a snort
of a good, solid pause
in the rope of your thoughts.

No, the thoughts insist, crowding
like sinners in a cauldron.
Is it me you're looking for?

WORRY DOLLS

Like a panel of judges, your six worry dolls are intently spread before you.

They are small and mostly male. They have legs, but don't have shoes. They have arms, but don't have hands. They have eyes and mouths, but don't have noses or ears. Their bodies are wrapped in threads of different colors: three purple pants, one white and one black; two green shirts, two orange and one red. The woman is dressed differently: she wears a three-color cloth wrapped as a skirt and blue thread wrapped as a shirt.

Everybody's head is covered with dangerous hair. You should not strike their heads or rub them together.

Being small does not diminish their powers. You can tell them anything. Pick up the first one and lay it on him. Pick up the next one and lay it on him.

Do not be greedy—one worry per doll and no more.

The six of them will lie quietly under your pillow until you fall asleep. After that, they will slither free and carry away your worries. One loads them on his back as though he is carrying a wardrobe. Another drapes them around his neck as though he has captured a large animal. The woman huddles her entrusted worry like a baby in her arms, and when it's too heavy, on her head, like a pot full of water.

The worry dolls walk as a group—awaiting one another, helping each other get up when someone slips along the way. (Keep in mind, it's dark out, and even darker where they are going.) It's a place far away. Twice removed from your life. There is nothing there but worries fetched by all the dolls around the world.

Curious things could be found in this place, if one dared go there.

Have you ever seen
a vulture
in a hurry?

Or a hawk
who didn't look
like a warrior?

Have you ever met
a deer who hated
her hunter?

Or a worm who didn't
try to find earth
twice as fast

after he was sliced in two?

YOU AND KARMA

for Ivan Metodiev

The sunflower and its seeds,
the donkey and its load,
the saint and his kindness

you shall know by their fruit.

Look—the sunflower
keeps on crying.
The donkey glows, and the saint
carries it in his arms.

FOOD

Tomatoes bring love.
Potatoes raise consciousness.

Onions spring compassion.
Mulberries promote change.

Corn is a generous mother.
Artichokes are modest knights.

You cannot love thy neighbor
without eating your vegetables.

You can stop world wars
with the kindness of a single fruit cup.

NOTES

"Do you mean" : "глупав" is a Bulgarian word and means "stupid."

"My tongue, my enemy" : This poem was first written in Bulgarian and instead of the Bulgarian word for "arrowhead," I used the word "боздуган," a word of Turkish origin which means a club-type weapon with spikes, akin to a mace.

"Cyrillic Letters" :
"АБВГДЕЖЗИЙКЛМНОПРСТУФХЦЧШЩЪЬЮЯ" is comprised of all the letters of the Bulgarian alphabet.

"Visit" : "tarator" is a typically Bulgarian cold summer soup with main ingredients of cucumbers and plain yogurt.

"The Artist" : Simeon Kondev is an artist, writer, and illustrator originally from Bulgaria.

"Beneath the skull—locked door" : Laurie Clewett is a poet living and working in Lexington, Kentucky.

"You and Karma" : Ivan Metodiev (1946-2003) is a beloved Bulgarian poet who wrote about God and Nature.

ACKNOWLEDGMENTS

My heartfelt gratitude to Dan, Simeon, all my friends and teachers. Deep appreciation to poet and publisher Larry W. Moore for his selfless work.

I am thankful to the editors of the following magazines, in which these poems, sometimes in slightly different form, first appeared:

Barrow Street: Lullaby, How long have you been like this

Best Poem: The Most

Border Crossing: So, what did you learn

Cat's Figment: The Way I Used to Pray to St. Catherine

Colere: Visit

Dictum (in Bulgarian): I am dark and damp and scared, I pictured you younger, Skin, I respond to kindness

Факел Алманах (*Fakel Almanac*, in Bulgarian): An Hour After, The Suitcase, O & I, Two

Introduction to *Feral* (a chapbook by Patty Paine): My Tongue, My Enemy

Inch: I enjoy your company

Journal of Kentucky Studies: Cyrillic Letters, Your Fate Whispered in Your Ear, Retirees in the Gym

The Louisville Review: Creative Spurt

Margie: The Fish, the Net and the Fisherman

Mississippi Crow: Worry Dolls

Monolith: Wear me, said the word lifesaver

Open 24 Hours: To the Bugs Still Drowning in the Pool

Red Lion Square: Mermaid in the Cornfield

Still: The Journal: One should exercise caution

Жената днес (*Woman Today,* in Bulgarian): The Kiss of the Stone

Several of the poems included in *The Porcupine of Mind* are also part of the chapbook *The Most* (Finishing Line Press, 2010)

ABOUT THE AUTHOR

Katerina Stoykova-Klemer's first poetry book, the bilingual *The Air around the Butterfly* (Fakel Express, 2009), won the 2010 Pencho's Oak award, given annually to recognize literary contribution to contemporary Bulgarian culture. She is the author of *The Most* (Finishing Line Press, 2010) and *Indivisible Number* (Fakel Express, 2011, Bulgarian only). Katerina is the editor of *Bigger Than They Appear: Anthology of Very Short Poems* (Accents Publishing, 2011). In 2007, Katerina founded Poezia, weekly poetry and prose workshops open to the public and based in Lexington, Kentucky. She is the creator and host of *Accents*, a radio show for literature, art and culture on WRFL, 88.1 FM, Lexington. In January 2010, Katerina launched Accents Publishing. Born and raised in Bulgaria, Katerina writes, thinks and dreams in two languages and believes wherever she happens to be is her home.